NO LONGER PROPERTY OF
SEATTLE PUBLIC LIBRARY

BIOGRAPHIES OF DIVERSE HEROES

LIN-MANUEL MIRANDA

STEPHANIE GASTON

TABLE OF CONTENTS

Lin-Manuel Miranda 3

Glossary 22

Index 22

A Crabtree Seedlings Book

School-to-Home Support for Caregivers and Teachers

This book helps children grow by letting them practice reading. Here are a few guiding questions to help the reader with building his or her comprehension skills. Possible answers appear here in red.

Before Reading:

- What do I think this book is about?
  - *I think this book is about Lin-Manuel Miranda and what inspired him to write the Broadway musical* Hamilton.
  - *I think this book is about his many talents and accomplishments.*

- What do I want to learn about this topic?
  - *I want to learn what schools Lin-Manuel Miranda attended so he could learn to compose music and write a play.*
  - *I want to learn if Lin-Manuel Miranda faced any difficulties on his way to stardom.*

During Reading:

- I wonder why…
  - *I wonder why Lin-Manuel Miranda was inspired to write a hip-hop musical about Alexander Hamilton.*
  - *I wonder why Lin-Manuel Miranda chose to use diverse actors in the play* Hamilton.

- What have I learned so far?
  - *I have learned that Lin-Manuel Miranda's family is from Puerto Rico and that he was born in New York City.*
  - *I have learned that he saw his first Broadway musical at the age of 7.*

After Reading:

- What details did I learn about this topic?
  - *I have learned that Lin-Manuel Miranda also wrote and starred in the musical* In the Heights *that he wrote while attending college.*
  - *I have learned that his musical* Hamilton *received the Pulitzer Prize for Drama.*

- Read the book again and look for the glossary words.
  - *I see the word* **composer** *on page 3 and the word* **diverse** *on page 19. The other glossary words are found on page 22.*

LIN-MANUEL MIRANDA

Lin-Manuel Miranda is an award-winning actor, playwright, and **composer**.

Miranda is best known for the **Broadway** musicals *In the Heights* and *Hamilton*.

He wrote, composed, and starred in both musicals.

Miranda was born in New York City on January 16, 1980.

His family is from Puerto Rico and they lived in a Hispanic community.

Miranda saw his first Broadway musical at the age of 7.

He took part in drama programs in middle school and in high school.

Miranda studied theater and film at Wesleyan University.

He wrote his first musical, *In the Heights*, while attending college.

Theater on the campus of Wesleyan University

The musical is based on a neighborhood similar to the one Miranda grew up in.

The first production of *In the Heights* opened in 2005.

The musical made its Broadway debut in 2008.

In the Heights was turned into a film in 2021.

The **biography** of Alexander Hamilton inspired Miranda's next big musical.

Alexander Hamilton was one of the founding fathers of the United States.

Miranda wrote and composed a hip-hop musical about Hamilton's life.

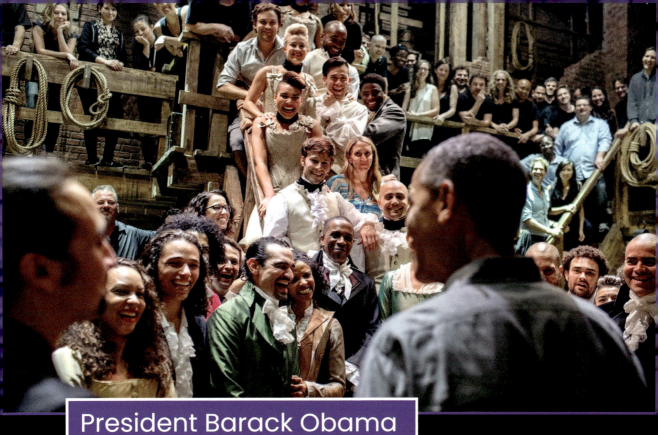

President Barack Obama met the cast of *Hamilton*.

The musical was praised for its **diverse** cast members.

Hamilton opened on Broadway in 2015 and was a huge success.

The musical won many awards, including the **Pulitzer Prize** for Drama.

Pulitzer Prize

Glossary

biography (bahy-og-ruh-fee): A written account of another person's life

Broadway (brawd-wey): A street in New York City, famous for its theaters

composer (kuhm-poh-zer): A person who writes music

diverse (dih-vurs): A range of people from different races, backgrounds, religions, and more

Pulitzer Prize (pool-it-ser prahyz): Annual prizes awarding outstanding achievements in journalism, literature, and music

Index

Broadway 4, 8, 14, 20

Hamilton 4, 18, 19, 20

Hamilton, Alexander 16, 17, 18

In the Heights 4, 10, 12, 14

Puerto Rico 6

Pulitzer Prize 20

Wesleyan University 10, 11

> "There's a million things I haven't done but just you wait. Just you wait."
>
> —Lin-Manuel Miranda

About the Author

Stephanie Gaston is a content producer for CNN and a screenwriter. She spent more than a decade working for the FOX and ABC affiliates in Miami, Florida, before joining the ranks at CNN in 2015, ahead of an unprecedented election cycle. Stephanie is a first-generation Haitian American who grew up in Fort Lauderdale, Florida, a diverse community with Latin and Caribbean influences. Throughout her career in journalism, Stephanie has covered major stories including presidential inaugurations, natural disasters, and royal weddings. Stephanie is a dog lover, movie buff, fitness enthusiast, and most importantly, a proud mom.

Written by: Stephanie Gaston
Designed by: Under the Oaks Media
Proofreader: Petrice Custance
Print coordinator: Katherine Berti

Photographs: Feature Flash: cover; Cuban Kite: p. 3; Allen G.: p. 5; JKS Studio: p. 7; Pitstock: p. 8; Monkey Business Images: p. 9; Steady John: p. 11; WENN: p. 13, 15; White House: p. 17, 19; Steve Jurvetson: p. 18; EQRoy: p. 21

Library and Archives Canada Cataloguing in Publication

Available at the Library and Archives Canada

Library of Congress Cataloging-in-Publication Data

Available at the Library of Congress

Crabtree Publishing Company
www.crabtreebooks.com   1-800-387-7650

Copyright © 2023 **CRABTREE PUBLISHING COMPANY**

All rights reserved. No part of this publication may be reproduced, stored in a retrieval system or be transmitted in any form or by any means, electronic, mechanical, photocopying, recording, or otherwise, without the prior written permission of Crabtree Publishing Company. In Canada: We acknowledge the financial support of the Government of Canada through the Canada Book Fund for our publishing activities.

Published in the United States
Crabtree Publishing
347 Fifth Avenue
Suite 1402-145
New York, NY, 10016

Published in Canada
Crabtree Publishing
616 Welland Ave.
St. Catharines, ON
L2M 5V6

Printed in the U.S.A./072022/CG20220201